The Next 30 Days

Days

A Journal for Moving Forward by Faith

SHARONDA LYNN

ISBN 978-0-578-75842-8

First Edition

Mountain Media Publishing
3401 Hartzdale Drive, Suite 103B
Unit #536
Camp Hill, PA 17011

www.theNXT30.com

Ordering Information:
Quantity sales. Special discounts are available on quantity purchases by corporations, associations, and others. For details, contact the publisher at the address above.

Cover and book design by Diggs Media, LLC at www.diggsmedia.co

Table of Contents

Dedication & Thanks

I would like to dedicate by book to the fighters and believers. Life hits us hard, but our bounce back is necessary. You are my heroes.

To my editors: Justin, Edquina, Tramona, Vernedine, and Shonyah. Without you, there is no way I would have accomplished the feat of getting this journal published. Your feedback and dedication were immeasurable. Love you guys.

And to my daughter, Khaliyah. You were the reason I always had a fighting spirit in me and the reason I kept going. Thank you for always giving your artistic assessment, even when it hurt. I am grateful to you and love you much.

How To Use This Journal

This is a suggestion of how to best use this journal and create a journaling environment. Trauma, loss, and other significant life events give us no warning when they will strike. This journal was created to ease the pain after you have experienced a major event in your life and you need balance. The following are suggestions to create an engaging journaling environment:

1. **Take time to breathe.** It is easy to sit down and start reading. However, we are not just reading. We are developing our best selves. The Bible says meditate both day and night. That means there is a metaphysical release of stress and information, a brain dump. Dump stress and welcome peace. Breathing exercises are excellent to refocus and promote relaxation. According to the University of Michigan's Michigan Medicine article, they suggest to do the following breathing exercise to de-stress:

   a. Sit in a comfortable position
   b. Put one hand on your belly below your ribs and one on your chest
   c. Take a deep breath in through your nose, and let your belly push out your hand. Your chest should not move.
   d. Breathe out through pursed lips like you are whistling.
   e. Repeat 3-10 times.

2. **Make sure you are in a decluttered space.** It is hard to do anything and truly be focused in a place of clutter. Pick a spot around you and set it up for

everyday journaling. Find a clean table, set the tone with candles or incense, and have enough space to allow for open books and studying.

3. **Dedicate Time to building you.** When I lost my job, I found myself busier outside the corporate world than inside the corporate world. It was unbelievable. Life will easily push your needs to the side. This is the time to say, "I deserve this and in this moment I come first." Make a date with yourself to journal and focus on healing your inner self.

Devotions

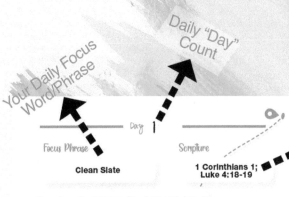

Your Daily Focus Word/Phrase

Daily "Day" Count

Scripture to read!

Day 1

Focus Phrase

Clean Slate

Scripture

**1 Corinthians 1;
Luke 4:18-19**

At our lowest points, we often believe that God is not there, not listening, and not interested. However, God calls each of us to a divine purpose to spread His Gospel. That does not mean that every man or woman will climb the pulpit. What it does mean is that there is PURPOSE sitting deep inside you, no matter what state you find yourself in right now.

Today, your slate is being wiped clean. Your sight is being recovered. Freedom is your blessing. Healing in your heart is certain. You are in the right place, at the right time, and God is ready for you.

Devotion and daily encouragement

Command Your Atmosphere

- I am called, sanctified by Christ.
- Everything I do will reflect my closeness to God.
- God chose me on purpose.

Daily declarations for success!

Daily Reflection

Think about where you are and where you hope to be. What challenges do you think are likely to come up? What can you think of that will counteract those challenges? (For example: A smoker generally loves to smoke but must quit. Counter-chews gum, indulges in hobbies, or starts a new venture to make sure smoking is not the first thing they think of in a quiet moment.)

Daily Reflections for Journaling

Your daily reflections are to inspire you to write. Use the next page to write your response.

Journal

Journal

Write about reflections and anything else on your mind.

Prayer Point

.God, cleanse my life from all wrongdoings that would stop my blessings.

Daily Prayer Point

Specific, Targeted Prayer.

LET'S GET STARTED

Focus Phrase

Clean Slate

Scripture

**1 Corinthians 1;
Luke 4:18-19**

At our lowest points, we often believe that God is not there, not listening, and not interested. However, God calls each of us to a divine purpose to spread His Gospel. That does not mean that every man or woman will climb the pulpit. What it does mean is that there is PURPOSE sitting deep inside you, no matter what state you find yourself in right now.

Today, your slate is being wiped clean. Your sight is being recovered. Freedom is your blessing. Healing in your heart is certain. You are in the right place, at the right time, and God is ready for you.

Command Your Atmosphere

- I am called, sanctified by Christ.
- Everything I do will reflect my closeness to God.
- God chose me on purpose.

Daily Reflection

Think about where you are and where you hope to be. What challenges do you think are likely to come up? What can you think of that will counteract those challenges? (For example: A smoker generally loves to smoke but must quit. Counter-chews gum, indulges in hobbies, or starts a new venture to make sure smoking is not the first thing they think of in a quiet moment.)

Prayer Point

God, cleanse my life from all wrongdoings that would stop my blessings.

Adopted in Love

Romans 8

Even though our present problems make us feel separated, we are not by ourselves. We are part of a family that extends beyond what we see or believe. Jesus was the first born, and He welcomed us into the family. In this family is true wealth. Not the wealth of dollars and cents. It is the wealth that speaks to wholeness and love.

Our lives as Kingdom Children provides us with the grace that lets us know that ALL things work for our good. Our destiny is attached to us just as we are attached to the Father. He will not let us down.

Command Your Atmosphere

- I am not condemned, I am free.
- What I allow my mind to think on is what I will live by.
- I am heir to the throne as a child of God with Jesus Christ.

Daily Reflection

Deferring to a Kingdom mindset removes you and puts all focus on God and His Will. What are some things you can identify as blockers or deterrents that make you feel separated from God and His family? What are one or two things that you can commit to releasing or putting aside?

Prayer Point

God created a family just for me. I am not alone.

Focus Phrase

Not Giving Up

Scripture

1 Corinthians 4

When troubles and challenges come it is NOT the time to give up. While you are going through your worst, it is still the opportunity to give your best. We often look like we are falling apart when God is developing us for a new life. Although people may think of you as ordinary, God adds the extra making you extraordinary.

Know that God is working when you are at your best and when you are at your worst. You are not conquered. God is rising in you even now.

Command Your Atmosphere

- God is working to bring new life in me.
- I will give my best and all will work to my advantage.
- What I see is temporary and what God has for me is eternal.

Daily Reflection

There are things that chip at your faith. What are some things that you are involved with that are weakening your faith? These items can include people, places, and/or activities. Remember, Little foxes spoil the vine. (For example: friends that seem positive, but their words leave you feeling low, less, or are centered on gossip.)

Prayer Point

God has not made me barren. I will be focused,
committed, and determined.

Humility

Proverbs 5

Many times our greatest failures happen because we are steeped in pride. We can feel prideful because we have money. We can feel prideful because we have a great skill. In this, we often miss God. We get so engulfed in different modes of foolishness that we end up giving away our blessing and others reap the rewards that we should reap.

God wants us to enjoy our life in the Kingdom. The path of pride and sin often seems right because they appeal to your inner sense. Do not fall into that trap. God does not miss a move we make. Our ways are before Him always.

Command Your Atmosphere

- I will take heed to and act on Godly wisdom.
- I will enjoy my life.
- I will live a disciplined life.

Daily Reflection

Often God gives us wisdom that we do not apply to our situation. What has God said to you that you need to apply to your life?

Prayer Point

God has not made me self-conceited, proud, or arrogant.

---- *Day* **5** ----

Focus Phrase

High Self Esteem

Scripture

2 Corinthians 12

Understanding that we are children of the living God will evoke many things. It can bolster your courage and it can order your steps. Many times that knowledge fosters a greater awareness of self, understanding that your status builds stature within you.

What being a child of God does not mean is that the tendrils of pride should take over. Instead, you are encouraged by God's adoption of you that all things are working for your favor and that you have a divine legacy.

Command Your Atmosphere

- I will speak the truth without boasting.
- God is my strength at all times.
- God will validate me.

Daily Reflection

Have you been in a position where people did not hold you in any esteem? I mean, nothing you did was ever right? Make a list today of all the things you do right.

Prayer Point

God created me in His image and I am strong in Him.

"Worry does not empty tomorrow of its sorrows; it empties today of its strength."

Corrie Ten Boom

Self-Control   **2 Timothy 1**

Many of the writings of the Apostle Paul came from a place of imprisonment. I am sure he felt virtual walls closing in on him daily. What kept him going was a desire to see the Word of God grow in everyone he could touch. Without self-control, he would have blended in with the pain and injustice he felt.

Many times we fixate on the problem or devastation we see before us. However, when you are called with a Holy Calling you should walk according to His purpose. Distractions are bound to come. Keep your resolve steady so that His good works will manifest through you.

Command Your Atmosphere

- I will not live in fear, but in power, love and a sound mind.
- I will control my emotional response.
- I will be bold with my God given gifts.

Daily Reflection

Life comes at us fast no matter who we are. What are some things that make you "lose" it? If you had control over your emotions, what could you accomplish soon that you are not already doing?

Prayer Point

God, allow me to function with total humility and
submission with my focus on you.

Faith in God   **Genesis 37**

When God gives dreams or visions, normally the have a purpose greater than anyone can comprehend. Always believe God at His Word. Have you ever heard the saying, "if it was something you could do in your power then you wouldn't need God for His?"

God is there when the people that you thought would be there are not. When you have God-size dreams, people will show you exactly who they are. People will envy the dream.
People will discourage the dream. People will hate you for the dream. God just need you to be strong enough to have faith in Him to be-lieve in the dream.

Command Your Atmosphere

- I will trust in God for every God-given vision.
- I will focus on God for His Word and sup-port.
- I will not put my trust in God.

Daily Reflection

Sometimes we just want to hear "Well Done" and our faith can be restored. Is there anything that you can think of stopping God from giving you a "Well Done" in any area?
(Including unforgiveness, lying, meanness, etc.)

Prayer Point

God has renewed my spirit to worship and praise Him in every situation.

Focus Phrase:

Scripture

Live Intentionally

Colossians 1

In a movie I watched, a young woman was going through rough times and was crying tremendously. It made the young woman immobile. Her friend came over and gave her a good pick-me-up speech. At the end of it, the friend saw that the talk was doing no good. So, the friend began to hit the young woman. And she kept hitting her until the young woman hit her back. The friend was happy because she felt the young woman was tired of being beat on and began to be intentional about fighting back.

In all things we must be intentional if we desire to get up, take our beds and walk. We may preach the Word of God and that we have Jesus, but ultimately our lives are proof of our intentions.

Command Your Atmosphere

- I will live intentionally.
- I will recognize and pray for the good works of others.
- I know God's Word is for me.

Daily Reflection

Intentional for you can mean many things. It can be being more organized, doing what you say you were going to do, or just showing up every day. How can you live more intentionally today?

Prayer Point

God, let my every move exude your purpose.

Glory is Coming   **1 John 3**

When things seem intense, it feels like our next step, venture, or idea just may be our last. But thank God that He is greater than that feeling of failure, disbelief, hurt, or pain. When we have confidence in God whatever we ask He will supply it according to His Word.

Every time you see a miracle, God has shown up. Every time the impossible happens, God has shown up. Even now, God is waiting to show up in your life. Invite Him in again and allow His glory to show up.

Command Your Atmosphere

- I am not a fugitive of the Kingdom but a child of its Creator.
- I abolish sin in my life and willingly love everyone.
- I will practice loving myself.
- I will not fail to ask for what I desire and need.

Daily Reflection

Often, we look for God to show up when we are not ready for Him to show up. Our God is timely, careful, and strategic in the way He places a load on us. Name one thing you can work on to be in better a position to receive God. Why did you choose it?

Prayer Point

God, prepare me to be your sanctuary that house the
power of your miracles.

Focus Phrase: *Scripture*

Energy & Excitement   **Ephesians 1**

You are lacking nothing from this point on. Every spiritual gift is given to those in Christ Jesus. That is something to be excited about. That means that this life you are living, you have the grace to live it. That dream you are dreaming, you have the grace to birth it. What an incredible charge!

It is important to direct your focus and energy on the blessings that have been decreed and confirmed over your life. You have been forgiven of your past and nothing can hold you back.

Command Your Atmosphere

- I am blessed with every spiritual blessing.
- I am totally loved by God.
- I have wisdom, revelation knowledge, a clear and focused understanding, and grasp this way of life.

Daily Reflection

Often when we are overburdened tiredness sets in. Do you notice any patterns that lead up to you feeling drained and/or lethargic? (For example: staying up late due to a problem, only to wake up early and be stuck on the same problem)

God is filling me with all power and authority to operate
in my sphere of excellence.

Prayer

Heavenly Father,

We never cease to say thank you. We never cease to give you glory. Allow the spirit of wisdom and revelation in the knowledge of you to increase. May our eyes be open to your understanding so that we may be receptors of your knowledge. You said that we have an inheritance. So let us focus our understanding on how you would have us to grow and to glow. Show your exceeding greatness of power toward your children, in Jesus name, amen.

God's Got You

Daniel 6

Many times we enter situations that test us or make us reconsider our purpose and reason. However, if you know without a shadow of a doubt that God set you on a path, the best thing you can do is follow the path. No one can do it for you. It was constructed and designed specifically for you.

In the same way, you cannot let fear grab hold. The funny thing about God is, His word cannot return void. It is in your future to win.

Command Your Atmosphere

- I have a spirit of excellence.
- I will stay true to building a relationship with God through prayer, fasting, & the Word.
- I will not beg or plead for acceptance.

Daily Reflection

It can be scary setting on an unknown path. Daniel did not know where his actions would lead him, but he did not let that sway him in any other direction. He stayed focused on the truth of God's word. What do you feel is leading you away from your purpose? Why?

Prayer Point

God does not make mistakes and has control of my
entire situation.

Build Your Faith   **Psalm 103**

There are special times in our lives when we are in seasons of flourish. Yet, we often hyper-focus on seasons of lack and disappointment, quickly forgetting we were just in a good space. It is very easy to focus on our pain and hurt when those feelings are magnified. However, instead of looking at a season negatively, zero in on what it is positively building in you. Is your faith in God growing? Is your ability to budget, reason, or navigate growing?

Men and women have many seasons that shape this journey we call life. The tough times serve to build our spiritual muscles. Our faith is developed when the storms are raging, not when they are at rest.

Command Your Atmosphere

- I know God answers all things.
- I will live, blossom, and flourish on this earth.
- I am covered under the Kingdom covenant of God.

Daily Reflection

When God is silent, we often mistake Him, thinking He is not there for us. However, silence can indicate building, learning, and growing. We have to cultivate our faith. What are 3 areas you need to build your faith in?

Every step I take, every mountain I climb, and every road
block I overcome is just a stepping stone for my destiny.

Great works are waiting for you

Philippians 1

Belief in a dream or vision takes guts. You have to be willing to not only take a step forward, but often you have to believe there is going to be fruit when it doesn't make sense. God is determined to finish the work He's started in you. He prophesied it, now it is up to you to believe it.

I pray that your efforts flourish, that you exceed your own expectations, and I pray you grow in both knowledge and discernment. As you step in your purpose, may the protection of Angelic hosts be working on your behalf. Great works are waiting for you. God said it. Believe in your ability to walk it out.

Command Your Atmosphere

- Grace is mine as a believer.
- My life and actions will incite Godly boldness.
- I will carry myself in a way that is worthy of the gospel and my good works will be on the lips of others.

Daily Reflection

There are some sneaky things that will hold you back from greatness. Fear is one. Are you afraid of what others may say or think? Do you have a fear of success? Write down your fears and find a scripture that says the opposite.

Prayer Point

God is building me for my future works.

Self-Control   **James 3**

We all stumble and mess up. We mess up in our relationships, in our homes, and on our jobs. However, we cannot allow ourselves to lose sight of our dreams because of a mistake. Mistakes are tools for growth.

Instead, be of good conduct. Get your work done. And be meek and a seeker of wisdom. Determine that today you will live well. You will live wisely. You will live humbly.

Command Your Atmosphere

- Even in my mess I will have self-control in words and deeds.
- I will not be a source of confusion and chaos.
- I will operate with good conduct, good works, and meekness.

Daily Reflection

When you look around, you will see the Grace of God helping you live. God's Grace is sufficient. What grace do you see the Lord applying to your life?

Journal

Prayer Point

God has created my mouth to be a tool and a power that
sends life to dead and broken situations.

Humility in ALL Things   John 5

It is easy to boast about what you are doing. We often do it when we are "trying to get our name out there." Instead of just saying this is what we do, we tell them this is how good we do it. There is a difference in promoting a business and promoting your achievements.

Let others and the word of God testify to who you are. We need the testimony of God's Word to solidify who we are and remind us of to be humble in our actions. People will often jockeyforpositionandsupporttheself-important before they believe the Word of God which says, "Your gift will make room for you." Your quiet can be loud too. Be humble. Let your actions speak before your mouth does.

Command Your Atmosphere

- I will focus on God, not people.
- I will let the work I do speak for itself.
- I will do as God commands without seek-ing the approval of man or becoming self-important.

Daily Reflection

Many times we let the pressures of others get to us. We feel the need to prove ourselves and we act according to that need. Instead we want to have our actions preprogrammed in our minds so that we do not act according to people but according to our own program (which should be God's program). What can you tweak so that the actions of people do not dictate your overall reaction?

Journal

Prayer Point

I have done nothing without the love and power of God.

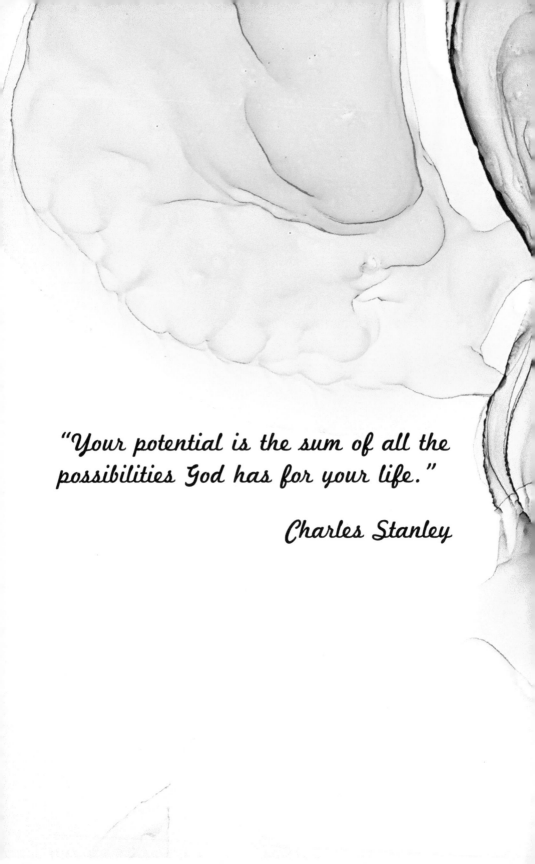

"Your potential is the sum of all the
possibilities God has for your life."

Charles Stanley

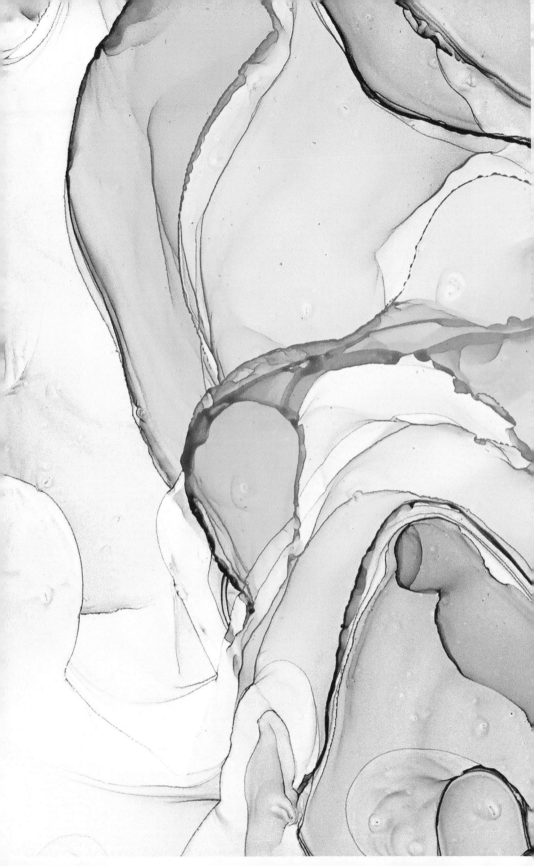

Focus Phrase

Stay Connected

Scripture

Genesis 13

Life will send circumstances your way and you will feel like all you can do is focus on the circumstance. Let us be very real here, it is often hard to remove your eyes from a difficult situation. However, trusting that God has things in control is a habit worth developing.

Things, situations, and challenges come yet there is a God in heaven that tells us if we focus on Him, we will be okay. In the end we win. In the end, God leads us. In the end, His success is our success. And that is what He needs us to understand. He would not lead us into anything less than success. So stay connected to God even when it does not make a lick of sense. Pray. Praise. Worship. Seek Him. He has your best interests at heart.

Command Your Atmosphere

- I will never stop praising and worshiping God.
- I will seek God's council in all things.
- I will stay connected to God's will and destiny for my life.

Daily Reflection

Many times it may feel like God is far away. It may feel like our prayers are disconnected. It is a trick of the enemy. There is purpose in the silence of God. There are answers, as well. What habits can you develop to help in times where God is quiet in your life?

Prayer Point

God, I will work with others as a team to achieve your purpose.

Contend

Jude 3

It is easier to do what our flesh wishes because it feels good. However, everything that feels good is not "God Good." Living by your flesh creates an atmosphere that encompasses a spirit of division when you are His.

We must build our faith and contend for our faith so that we are able to be in the love of God. There is protection, safety, healing and so much more in the love of God.

Command Your Atmosphere

- I will contend against all for my faith.
- I will not be self-serving, but I will keep myself in the love of God.
- I will not curse others in their process.

Daily Reflection

When we see other people straddling the faith, what is your reaction? Is it one of mercy and understanding? Or is it one of judgment? We must be tender with people and merciful with them. It is the sin that we is the problem, not the person. How can you step up your mercy and care of others that are struggling? How do you help them contend for their faith?

Prayer Point

God, I will not give up or give in unless you tell me to stop.

Preparation   ## 1 Thessalonians 4

Often people appear to be holy but are actually scandalous, especially when it comes to having sexual sins. It is an easy state to fall into. Let's face it, we want to do right, but wrong just might feel better. However, a wrong move at the right time can created ripples in your future that are hard to eradicate.

We want our character to line up with our mouths, so that we can ultimately dictate the flow of our future. God calls us to aspire to lead a life without sin and pettiness, minding our own business, and working with our own hands. We are then in preparation to live in a way that commands the respect of others and aligns us properly with God.

Command Your Atmosphere

- I will excel in the knowledge of the Kingdom of God.
- I will control my body and abstain from sexual sin.
- I will live a holy life and not defraud others.

Daily Reflection

In the delicateness of sexuality, we often look at one sexual sin greater than another. The truth is, it is all sin if it is outside of God's plan. If you are single, what are you doing to combat sexual urges that are not fit for the Kingdom of God? If you are married, how can you enhance your intimacy with your partner? If you are married and in sexual sin, what steps can you take to get back on track?

———————— • Journal • ————————

Prayer Point

God, as you prepare me, create in me a clean heart and renew a right spirit.

Focus Phrase

Stay the course

Scripture

Galatians 5

What is your work saying about you? Does it say you are consistent? Does it say you are timely? Or, does it say you are something more negative like careless, untrustworthy, and undependable? What you do speaks louder than any words you have to say.

The enemy comes to take away your good works that speak on your behalf. Stay the course. God is still working on you. You are good fruit.

Command Your Atmosphere

- I will not go backward.
- I will walk in the spirit and be led by the spirit.
- I will exhibit good fruit and be eligible for the Kingdom of God.

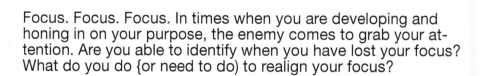

Daily Reflection

Focus. Focus. Focus. In times when you are developing and honing in on your purpose, the enemy comes to grab your attention. Are you able to identify when you have lost your focus? What do you do {or need to do} to realign your focus?

Prayer Point

My eyes are focused on the will and unction of God.

A clean heart & right spirit

1 John 2

Reflection is often the key that unlocks mysteries. We never know why things keep happening the way they do repeatedly until we begin to examine the cause and response to each problem.

Without reflection, history is destined to continually repeat itself. Whatever you want to do or need to do should be the reflection of what is on the inside of you. Meaning, if you want to be successful believe that success is already inside you. If you want to show love, the love of God must be inside you.

Command Your Atmosphere

- I am anointed by the Holy one and recognize Him on the inside of me.
- I declare and testify to the truth of Jesus Christ.
- I will let my light shine so that I will not be a stumbling block to others.

Daily Reflection

What are you reflecting? Do you have a clean heart and a right spirit? What, if anything, can you modify so that your presentation to others is what you desire?

Prayer Point

I will renew my mind so that I am able to stay in the mind of Christ.

Father, we bow our knees to you and acknowledge your might and greatness. May Christ dwell in our hearts through faith. May we be able to comprehend the size and depth of your love for us. And, may we be filled with the fullness of you, God.
In Jesus Name,
Amen.

Peace be unto You   **Matthew 5**

In your journey, people are going to be upset by your walk and faith. Do not think about them. Leave your enemies and haters alone. Keep at your goals until you get the results you are looking for. Your work will speak more after you complete it.

Jesus did not stop. He kept going to completion. When He saw a need, he met the need. Do not cower when it is time to meet the need. Be careful of what you say when the need is presented and be consistent and authentic in who you are.

Command Your Atmosphere

- I will not stop trying to get to my destiny.
- I will remain humble in actions and speech.
- I will be authentic about what I feel and do.
- I will continue to grow my faith and be a solution.

Daily Reflection

What fears are holding you back? Do you feel afraid to take on your future? Make a list of things you feel are a weight. Beside them, write actionable steps that will allow you to overcome them. Then, check the items off the list as you crush them.

Journal

Prayer Point

On my worst day, as well as, on my best, I will find the
peace of God and keep moving forward.

Focus Phrase

Scripture

Divine Protection

Matthew 8

When you think of Divine Protection, what rises in your mind? Sometimes the things that challenge us and makes us beg for divine protection, is often fear. Fear will cloud all direction.

The problem is, when we are following Christ and His will for our lives, we must leave our comfort zone. It frequently feels awkward, but do not let your first response be full of emotion or fear. Let it be filled with faith. Faith makes you fearless. God makes you win.

Command Your Atmosphere

- I will have great faith.
- I will leave my comfort zone for the Kingdom of God.
- I will not tremble in emotions or fear when challenges rise.

Daily Reflection

What do you think your next step should be? What is God pushing you to work on, complete, or be open to? If you thought it was possible, what are the steps you would take to make it happen?

Prayer Point

My battles are fought and won by a God that never gives up.

**Your Purpose is Your
Reason**

John 15

Purpose. One of the most elusive things in life. The Word says, we can ask for what we need and desire with an expectation of receiving it. The easiest way to get an understanding about your purpose is to ask God. However, we often forget to ask.

You can ask God anything and get the answer you are seeking. You are part of a divine family. You are grafted in to bear much fruit. God wants you to live your best life and prosper. Ask and He will answer.

Command Your Atmosphere

- I am connected to the vine through Jesus Christ.
- I am loved and give love and joy.
- I will bear fruit and God will be glorified.
- I will ask for what I need from God with expectation.

Daily Reflection

Do you hear from God or do you feel He does not talk to you anymore? When you ask God for an answer, give Him time to respond. What is your most pressing needs? Write them down and expect them to be answered as you pray over them.

Prayer Point

God, every gift, calling, and anointing I have are set
aside and developed for your purpose.

Learn the System   **Luke 19**

Everything has a system. It can be a system of order, or a system of disorder. Many times the systems that God has called us to does not make us happy. Your feelings will often find themselves in an unhappy state.

However, seize the God opportunity regardless. Shift your focus. Many people miss out on great opportunities because they want to feel good. Your worth is not measured in feel good situations. Your worth is measure when peace has left and the storm rages.

Command Your Atmosphere

- I will do great works with my hands regardless of who's authority I must be submitted to.
- I will recognize God in all things.
- I will seize the opportunity and allow God to direct the rest.

Daily Reflection

Some of the most trying moments offer the greatest reward. What are some things that make you want to give up? How can you overcome each one?

Prayer Point

There are Godly systems and ungodly systems that I will
identify and understand.

Be Kind

Luke 10

Everyone's process is different. I am reminded of homeless people and their individual stories. You have never seen a child say they wanted to be homeless when they grew up. I look at these people and wonder at their lives and resiliency.

Not everybody looks at the homeless in a positive manner. People can be cruel when some are going through a process that does not resemble their own processes. Be sensitive enough to be kind to others. Remember, Christ on the inside of us loves everyone.

Command Your Atmosphere

- I will be smart and safe as I do the Lord's work.
- I will bless a servant of God with a measure of gratitude.
- I will not push God on the unwilling.

Daily Reflection

Did you know that for you to do the work God has appointed you to do that He will give you authority over it? God has blessed you to win. If you knew that you were going to win, what are some things you would do?

Prayer Point

I will have compassion for the plight of others.

"God never said that the journey would be easy,

but He did say that the arrival would be worthwhile."

Max Lucado

Be Dynamic and Faithful   **Psalm 91**

Funny how knowing that you will win can change how you think about your life. It was not until I allowed God in every aspect of my life, that I saw the God who delivers, covers, sends fear running, and protects.

Do not shield yourself from God. Instead, make Him your dwelling place. Talk to Him about your struggles. When He sees your dependency on Him, he will make sure you are secure in His fortress where there is refuge.

Command Your Atmosphere

- God and I are in fellowship.
- God is my strength, covering, protection, and deliverer.
- God's truth is my shield, and nothing can overcome me.

Daily Reflection

We all have quirks. Those quirks are what keeps us unique and dynamic. Have you ever hidden yourself to fit in? Are you still doing it? Why or Why not?

Prayer Point

I will be a dynamic light that will attract many things and
I will remain faithful to my God.

Trust and Fear not for I am with you

Psalm 55

Do you really trust God to be on your side? To trust God, is to trust Him in good times and bad times. Yes, bad times. Uncertain times are the perfect time for God to show up and blow your mind.

Ask God to deal with the good and the bad. Allow him to take care of everything. Take your hands off the wheel and allow God to drive. He is delighted to take care of you.

Command Your Atmosphere

- I will seek the council of God first.
- I will ask God to take care of my enemies and silence their tongue.
- God will hear my voice and redeem me in peace.
- I am God's and I will not fall to ruin.

Daily Reflection

Have you felt blocked? Have you had some hard times? Are you struggling in areas of wealth and success? Have you taken it to God? Write Him a love letter and tell Him all about it.

Journal

Prayer Point

I will trust and believe that God will not allow me to fail in
all that He has called me to.

**Project Who You
Represent**

Ephesians 2

God give grace for salvation. We are therefore free from sin and wrath when we become Kingdom citizens. That is why it is super important to show ourselves as God's children.

Who we represent directs how we walk, talk, operate, and drive? If you want to be known as great, reflect the Great God you serve. That same power to love, help, and teach that Jesus had rests in you.

Command Your Atmosphere

- I am alive and converted by God.
- I am raised up to the life and order of Heaven as a citizen.
- I have power to overcome sin and darkness.

Daily Reflection

Authenticity is so underrated in the world. People rather go with a flock of pigeons than to be the only black bird. What are some great things that make you unique? Do they line up with the Word of God?

Prayer Point

I am made in the likeness of a King and I will act like I am His heir.

Simply because "I AM"   **2 Timothy 4**

Life is like a box of chocolates. Just like a box of chocolates, life has variety. It is amazing when you think about it. Some of the chocolate we love. Others, we dislike and are happy to give away. But ultimately, it is a gift that gives over and over again. Just like life.

In life, there will always be ups and downs, good and bad. Be encouraged to keep fighting, finish the race, and keep the faith. Always remain humble and ask for help. God will stand with you, strengthen you and deliver you from every evil work.

Command Your Atmosphere

- I will endure, keep my head up, and fulfill the purpose in my life.
- I will fight the good fight, keep the faith, and finish the race.
- I will ask for help when I find myself in need.
- I am delivered and preserved from every evil work.

Daily Reflection

The great "I AM" is calling you out of the darkness into His marvelous light. Your testimony will change lives. In a short paragraph or two, list the things that stand out in your testimony that can help someone else who reads it.

Prayer Point

I serve a God that is all powerful and can do anything.

Honor God   **Joshua 8**

Did you know that in the end, you win? Oh yeah, you do. When God sends you on a mission, it is not just your mission. It is a divine setup. We don't serve a losing God. We serve a winning God. Wherever He sends you is a sure enough win.

So here is to your every provision being met, your hard times rewarded, and your cup running over. Goodness and mercy is packing their bags to follow you, and the direction of God will lead you. No fear in this next level. No fear in this next step. God will bless your plans, but you need to know that the challenges that come are already pre-won.

Command Your Atmosphere

- I will not fear where God has sent me.
- What God commands, I will do.
- I am a person of valor and I am ready.
- I am victorious and I am reaching every goal.

Daily Reflection

Have you prayed about your next step? Write down your prayer and if you have it, a plan of action.

_____ Journal _____

Prayer Point

My actions, my words, and my thoughts will bring honor
to God.

Prayer

Lord, you are great and mighty. You make all things new. We thank you in advance for all that you do. We testify that we will no longer walk as the rest of the world in small thinking and small understanding. We come away from dark thinking and dark understanding. We reject living a life that is alienated from you, God. Thank you for filling us with intelligence and transparency. Thank you for protecting us from lewdness and greed. Today, we put away all that concerned us in the past... all the contempt... all the negativity, and are renewed in the spirit of our minds. We put on a new man, created by God to exemplify righteousness and holiness. We glorify you for the "new" you are bringing our way, in Jesus name, Amen.

Command Your Atmosphere

Everyday you have 3-5 declarations for commanding your atmosphere. All the declarations are based on the scripture reading for that day. We thought it would be amazing for you to be able to access them in one place.

Day 1
I am called, sanctified by Christ.
Everything I do will reflect my closeness to God.
God chose me on purpose.

Day 2
I am not condemned, I am free.
What I allow my mind to think on is what I will live by.
I am heir to the throne as a child of God with Jesus Christ.

Day 3
God is working to bring new life in me.
I will give my best and all will work to my advantage.
What I see is temporary and what God has for me is
    eternal.

Day 4
I will take heed to and act on Godly wisdom.
I will enjoy my life.
I will live a disciplined life.

Day 5
I will speak the truth without boasting.
God is my strength at all times.
God will validate me.

Day 6
I will not live in fear, but in power, love and a sound mind.
I will control my emotional response.
I will be bold with my God given gifts.

Day 7
I will trust in God for every God-given vision.
I will focus on God for His Word and support.
I will not put my trust in God.

Day 8
I will live intentionally.
I will recognize and pray for the good works of others.
I know God's Word is for me.

Day 9
I am not a fugitive of the Kingdom but a child of its
    Creator.
I abolish sin in my life and willingly love everyone.
I will practice loving myself.
I will not fail to ask for what I desire and need.

Day 10
I am blessed with every spiritual blessing.
I am totally loved by God.
I have wisdom, revelation knowledge, a clear and
    focused understanding, and grasp this way of life.

Day 11
I have a spirit of excellence.
I will stay true to building a relationship with God through
    prayer, fasting, & the Word.
I will not beg or plead for acceptance.

Day 12

I know God answers all things.

I will live, blossom, and flourish on this earth.

I am covered under the Kingdom covenant of God.

Day 13

Grace is mine as a believer.

My life and actions will incite Godly boldness.

I will carry myself in a way that is worthy of the gospel
and my good works will be on the lips of others.

Day 14

Even in my mess I will have self-control in words and
deeds.

I will not be a source of confusion and chaos.

I will operate with good conduct, good works, and
meekness.

Day 15

I will focus on God, not people.

I will let the work I do speak for itself.

I will do as God commands without seeking the approval
of man or becoming self-important.

Day 16

I will never stop praising and worshiping God.

I will seek God's council in all things.

I will stay connected to God's will and destiny for my life.

Day 17

I will contend against all for my faith.

I will not be self-serving, but I will keep myself in the love
of God.

I will not curse others in their process.